THE MILITARY EXPERIENCE.

Special Operations:
SEARCH AND RESCUE

THE MILITARY EXPERIENCE.
Special Operations:
SEARCH AND RESCUE

DON NARDO

MORGAN REYNOLDS
PUBLISHING

GREENSBORO, NORTH CAROLINA

The Military Experience.
Special Operations: Search and Rescue
Copyright © 2013 by Morgan Reynolds Publishing

Library of Congress Cataloging-in-Publication Data

Nardo, Don, 1947-
 Special operations : search and rescue / by Don Nardo.
    p. cm. -- (The military experience)
 Includes bibliographical references.
 ISBN 978-1-59935-362-3 -- ISBN 978-1-59935-363-0 (e-book) 1.
United
States. Air Force--Search and rescue operations. 2. United States. Air
Force--Parachute troops--Juvenile literature. 3. Special forces
(Military
science)--United States. I. Title.
 UG633.N28 2012
 358.4--dc23
                                        2012024008

Printed in the United States of America
First Edition

Book cover and interior designed by:
Ed Morgan, navyblue design studio
Greensboro, NC

Table of Contents

Navy SEALs exit a helicopter before securing the beach during a capabilities demonstration at the annual East Coast SEAL reunion.

CHAPTER ONE

Navy SEALs demonstrate a special patrol insertion/
extraction from an MH-60S Seahawk helicopter
during a capabilities demonstration as part of the
2009 Veterans Day ceremony and Muster XXIV
at the National Navy UDT-SEAL Museum in Fort
Pierce, Florida.

A Daring RESCUE Above the Clouds

Mount McKinley, Alaska

One day in 1991, Kim Hong Bim suddenly became involved in a horrifying fight for his life. A Korean man who loved scaling mountains, he thought he was up to climbing Mount McKinley. Located in central Alaska, it rises an astonishing 20,320 feet (6,194 m) into the sky. That makes it the tallest mountain in North America. Bim was a strong, tough climber. But on this particular day he wasn't quite strong enough. Reaching the three-quarter mark of the climb, he became heavily fatigued. Soon he passed out and the biting cold began to drain his body of warmth.

Fortunately for Bim, some of the world's best-trained rescuers happened to be on the mountain that day. Jack Brehm and a handful of colleagues were camped at a spot about 3,000 feet (915 m) below Bim's location. Someone in an airplane had spotted Bim's motionless body. And soon afterward Brehm had gotten a radio call asking if he could help. He and his men were members of one of the U.S. Air Force's special ops, or commando teams: the Pararescue Jumpers, often called the PJs for short. Each year they rescue hundreds of people caught in dire, life-threatening situations.

This time, Brehm later recalled, the situation was almost beyond dire. He later called it "my hairiest mission." First, they were situated in a place so high and remote, it was above the clouds. The air was very thin, making it hard to breathe. Also, it was bone-chillingly cold. Moreover, Brehm and his fellow PJs were already exhausted from their own climb. Finally, they did not have all the equipment they normally carried when going out on a mission.

THE LINE BETWEEN RESCUER AND "RESCUEE"

This did not stop Brehm and the others from immediately going to Bim's aid. "It took us 11 hours to climb to him," Brehm later said. "When we got there, we discovered he was critical. He was unconscious and had been a little over two days. So we needed to get him down as soon as possible."

The rescuers realized that taking Bim down the mountain the same way they had climbed up would take too long. Nearby they spied a crack that led to a high vertical cliff. So they decided to attach ropes to the stricken man and lower him straight down the cliff face. They had to move fast because of worsening weather. "The temperature was going down," Brehm recalled. "And the winds were picking up to around 60 miles per hour on the ridge we were on."

Then something unexpected and scary happened. With Bim and two of the PJs hanging in the air thousands of feet above the ground, they ran out of rope. Even worse, by this time Brehm and his men were on the edge of total exhaustion. "There is a fine line always in every mission between rescuer and rescuee," Brehm later said:

Specialist Dave Shebib attempts to reach the summit of Mount McKinley, also known as Denali, in Alaska's Denali National Park and Preserve.

And you don't ever want to cross that line. We found ourselves right on the brink, where in a matter of minutes we were going to cross the line where *we* were going to need rescue. So [we] made the right call. [We decided] to get ourselves dug in, get some food, get in some tents, [and] get warmed up. [We got] a tent erected [and] got some stoves lit. We got fluids [into our bodies].

THAT OTHERS MAY LIVE

After eating, drinking, and resting, Brehm and the others managed to get their patient the rest of the way down the mountain. Kim Hong Bim lived to climb other mountains. Thereafter, he felt indebted to the PJs who had saved him from certain death.

fact BOX

The Undaunted Bim

Although Kim Hong Bim was rescued from his Mount McKinley dilemma, the cold badly damaged his fingers. So he lost them all. This did not end his climbing career, however. Fitted with artificial hands, the undaunted Bim went on to reach the summit of Mount Everest, the world's tallest peak.

Air Force pararescuemen like Brehm are part of only one of several U.S. military groups called special ops. That term is short for Special Operations Forces (SOF). The members of the various SOF groups complete missions that are usually too difficult for ordinary soldiers. Other U.S. special ops groups include the Army's Green Berets and Rangers; the Navy's famous SEALs; and the members of the Marines' Special Operations Command.

Of these, a few Navy and Marine units are trained to rescue people in difficult circumstances. But the Air Force's PJs are the military's primary special ops rescue force. The U.S. Coast Guard also has a number of expert rescuers, although most are not labeled special ops. Whether they belong to the Air Force or Coast Guard, these professional rescuers regularly risk their lives for others. They selflessly and proudly live up to their motto— "That others way live."

The United States Air Force Pararescue Badge

U.S. Air Force pararescuemen conduct a parachute training jump from an HC-130 aircraft over Djibouti, Africa.

The rescue of plane crash victims during World War II along the China-Burma border (*circled on the map*) inspired the formation of a group of rescuers that later became the Air Force's Pararescue Jumpers.

The First Pararescuemen

The U.S. military did not always have specially trained rescuers. The first appeared during World War II (1939-1945), in which the United States and other Allies fought the Germans and Japanese. The Air Force suddenly saw a need for units that could rescue pilots who had crashed. So it began to train men for such units. In Europe, the American 5th Emergency Rescue Squadron (ERS) emerged. Special rescuers were also badly needed in the Asian sector of the war. In 1943, an Allied plane carrying twenty-one people went down near the China-Burma border. A number of injured survivors were trapped in a remote region behind enemy lines. Some U.S. soldiers with medical knowledge volunteered to parachute into the crash site. They did so and saved the lives of the victims. Not long after the end of the war, the Air Force established a formal unit of such men. Able to fight, parachute, and heal the injured, they were the first pararescuemen.

CHAPTER TWO

U.S. Navy SEALs participate in tactical warfare training.

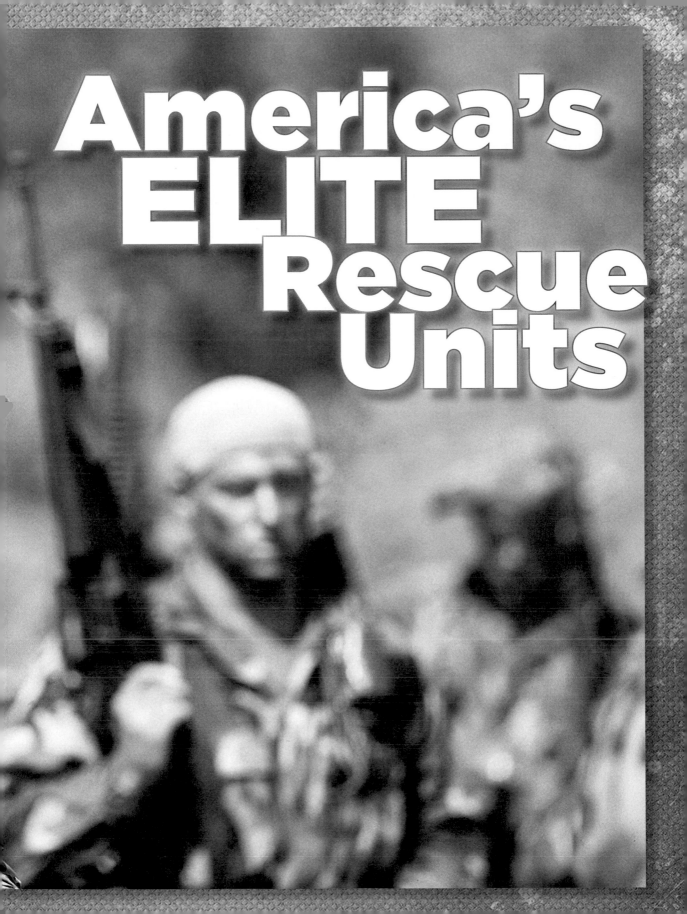

America's ELITE Rescue Units

The U.S. military's primary special ops rescuers are the Air Force's pararescuemen, or PJs. They are among the nation's most multitalented professionals. Each year they save the lives of soldiers, sailors, and other military personnel. They also rescue civilians. And they often do this under very dangerous or even violent conditions.

These top-notch rescuers are surprisingly few in number. Only about 450 of them are on active duty at present. And the word *active* must be stressed here. Between 2001 and 2011, they carried out more than 12,000 rescues, some at sea and others on land.

fact BOX

Rescuing Astronauts

Some of the Air Force's pararescuemen were happy to put their swimming and scuba-diving skills to a special use. They did so at the end of the U.S. space agency NASA's Gemini 8 space flight in the 1960s. When the astronauts aboard the capsule splashed down in the sea, three PJs rescued them.

Astronauts Neil Armstrong (*left*) and David Scott sit with their spacecraft hatches open while awaiting the arrival of the recovery ship, the USS *Leonard F. Mason* after the successful completion of their Gemini 8 mission. They are assisted by U.S. Navy divers.

U.S. Air Force Airman Matthew Bernard (*foreground*) wears a water-filled mask while performing flutter kicks during an extended training day at the Pararescue Indoctrination Training Center at Lackland Air Force Base in Texas.

A WIDE RANGE OF SKILLS

To accomplish these missions, the elite Air Force rescuers undergo extremely difficult and thorough training. It gives them a wide range of skills that frequently end up helping the victims they rescue to survive. One of the most important of these skills is an expertise in first aid and other medical treatments. This allows the rescuers to keep injured victims alive long enough to get them to a hospital.

The use of the rescuers' other skills depends on the situation, which varies from mission to mission. Sometimes they must reach and/or evacuate a victim through water. So all pararescuemen become skilled swimmers and scuba divers. Other times the victims are on mountain slopes, in forests or jungles, or in deserts. The special ops rescuers are adept at surviving in all of those settings. Retired PJ John Cassidy summed up the many abilities of the members of his profession. He also pointed out their importance to society, proudly saying:

> Pararescue is the singular most potent military occupation dedicated to the rescue and recovery of aircrews downed in an area of conflict. [Also] Pararcscuemen adapt to the physical conditions surrounding the survivor and [are able to do their jobs in] adverse areas and conditions to aid and recover distressed and injured personnel. . . . It is the US Air Force Pararescue specialty that melds the skills of other professions—medicine, survival, parachuting, combat swimmer, and [others]—into a unique capability that deals with the many problems and dangers facing rescue, [all so] "that others may live."

TO GET THE GOOD GUY OUT

The men of the Air Force's pararescue units have one crucial added skill. At times, they must protect the victims while an enemy is firing at them. As a result, the PJs are trained in combat, as other special ops personnel are. This means that an elite rescuer is sometimes forced to kill one person in order to save another. One pararescueman remarked:

> We want to get in and get out [of a mission] . . . no fuss, no muss. But we're not going to raise the white flag the first time the enemy says "boo!" either. We're just as skilled in taking lives as we are at saving them. And sometimes you have to do bad stuff to get the good guy out.

Whether they work in combat situations or not, the pararescuemen give their all in each and every mission. They are professional, dedicated, and unselfish. As a PJ who fought in Vietnam put it, "Being part of this team is a joy in your life that no amount of money can buy."

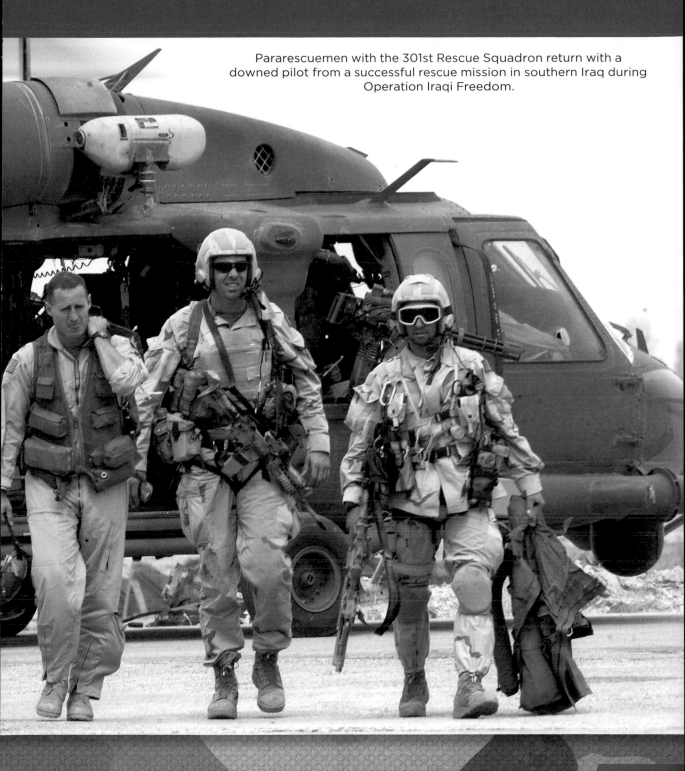

Pararescuemen with the 301st Rescue Squadron return with a downed pilot from a successful rescue mission in southern Iraq during Operation Iraqi Freedom.

The Always Watchful Coast Guard Rescuers

In addition to the PJs, many non-special ops Search and Rescue (SAR) units exist in the United States. Of these, the most numerous and famous are those who serve in the U.S. Coast Guard. This branch of the military was officially established in 1915. Today it has about 42,000 men and women on active duty. Several thousand of them are involved in SAR operations in the nation's waterways on a regular basis.

The overall aims of the Coast Guard's rescue units are best stated by the Coast Guard itself:

> The ultimate goal of the Coast Guard's SAR program is to prevent loss of life. . . . Our success in meeting this goal is the result not only of how well the SAR system responds to maritime SAR incidents. [It is] also the [result of the] efforts of other maritime safety programs, including recreational boating safety and commercial vessel safety.

Coast Guard SAR teams around the country are almost constantly busy. Those stationed at Elizabeth City, North Carolina, alone average almost 360 missions each year. Since that station was established, its personnel have rescued or assisted more than 10,000 people. Other Coast Guard rescue teams helped the survivors of Hurricane Katrina in the Gulf of Mexico region in 2005. In the wake of record flooding, they plucked people off of rooftops. They also went into flooded neighborhoods and saved stranded homeowners. More than 4,000 residents were rescued in only the first week following the hurricane.

Although not designated special ops, Coast Guard rescuers are extremely well trained. They are also highly dedicated to helping others. They remain always watchful for distress calls from boaters and others in need of immediate assistance.

U.S. Coast Guard Petty Officer 2nd Class Shawn Beaty looks for survivors of Hurricane Katrina, as he flies in an HH-60J Jayhawk helicopter over New Orleans. Katrina, packing 145-mile-an-hour winds as it made landfall on August 29, 2005, ranks as one of the five deadliest hurricanes in U.S. history.

CHAPTER THREE

Students from Basic Underwater Demolition/ SEAL (BUD/S) Class 287 participate in night gear exchange during the second phase of training at the Naval Amphibious Base, Coronado, in California.

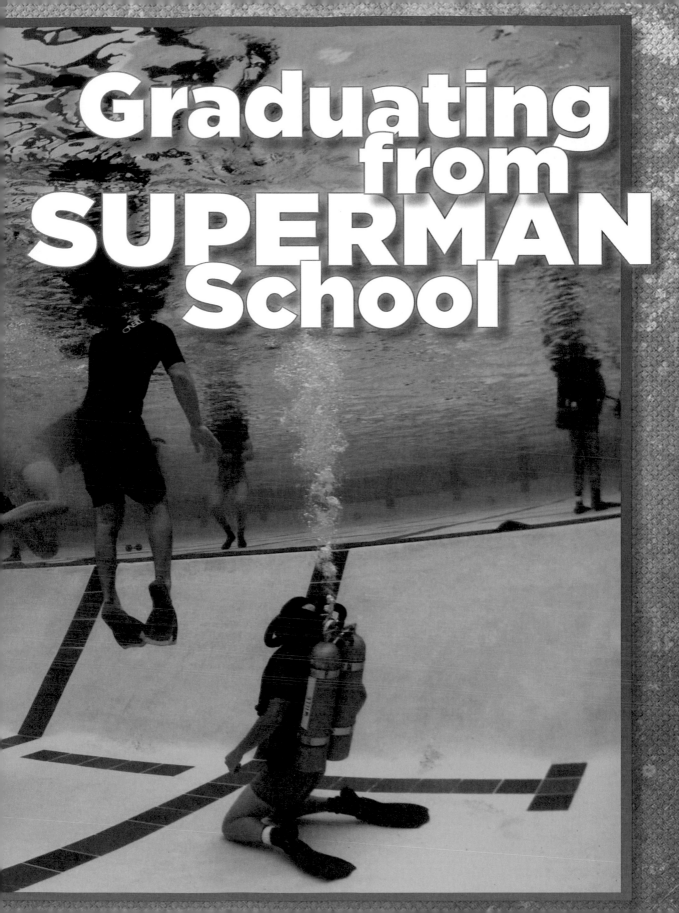

Graduating from SUPERMAN School

There are several reasons that the U.S. military's special ops rescuers are so successful so often. Chief among them is their extensive training. It includes physical conditioning on a par with that of the Navy SEALs and Army Green Berets. It also consists of a wide range of courses that teach important skills. The recruits in the program do not have a choice of which courses to take, as regular college students do. A would-be pararescueman must take and pass all the courses. If he fails even one, he cannot graduate.

CRACKING THE STUDENTS OPEN

There is no single, central school for pararescue recruits. Instead, the courses in the program are taught at military bases across the country.

Together, they are called "the Pipeline," as described here by PJ Jack Brehm:

> "The Pipeline" is just a series of schools that you have to go through to become a qualified para-rescueman. It takes about 18 months. . . . They take in about 80 students and they tell you on day one they will graduate eight. Eight will be the maximum they will graduate. . . . You know on day one there is a 90 percent chance you will be washed out of the training at some point. . . . It just gets tougher and tougher and tougher until there are eight [or fewer men] left.

This high failure rate clearly shows the extreme difficulty of the courses in the Pipeline program. Another indication of how hard the training is comes from statements made by some of the teachers. Master Sergeant Steve Sanko, an instructor at the military's combat divers school in Key West, Florida, said:

> We want to break the students down, crack them open, and peek inside them to see what they're made of. . . . We want to find out if they're quitters. Without drive and determination, you'll fail the mission. If you fail in the [training] pool, no problem. We'll drag you out and send you home. But fail on a mission and you come home in a body bag.

Masks full of water, the new Marine Combat Diver class signals "OK" as the instructor passes. New students are trained to clear water from a mask, even at the bottom of the ocean.

THE FIRST PHASE

The first stage of the Pipeline consists of an introductory course sometimes called Team Training. Lasting two months, it stresses physical conditioning and gets the recruits into tip-top shape. To this end, they do a grueling series of sit-ups, push-ups, running, and pool work (water-based exercises) each day.

Simply to pass this phase of the training, the recruits must accomplish some basic minimums. For example, they must be able to do fifty sit-ups in two minutes and fifty push-ups in the same amount of time. They also must complete a 1.5 mile (2.4 km) run in under ten minutes, thirty seconds. In the pool, they have to swim 1,640 feet (500 m) in fewer than sixteen minutes. And they must swim 66 feet (20 m) under water without coming up for air.

Trainees prepare for push-ups with their Basic Crewman Training (BCT) classmates at the Naval Amphibious Base, Coronado. BCT is the first phase of the Special Warfare Combatant-craft Crewmen (SWCC) Pipeline.

WATER TORTURE AND MORE

After leaving the introductory course, students in the Pipeline move on to the four-week-long combat diving phase. Air Force Master Sargeant Pat McKenna provides this brief overview:

> Pool week runs the first seven days, and to some, may look like water torture. If you survive treading water with a 16-pound belt or bobbing for precious breaths with your hands tied behind your back with feet bound, instructors then tie knots in your regulator hose, tear off your mask and harass you underwater. . . . To pass the course, pararescuemen must complete a 3,000-meter [9,840 foot] underwater navigation swim.

In the many months that follow, the recruits pass through several more phases and courses. In one, they learn to escape a sinking aircraft and swim to safety through ice-cold water. In another they become proficient at parachuting from planes at varying heights above the ground.

Next, the recruits receive instruction in how to evade enemy capture and to escape from an enemy camp. Still another course teaches the recruits how to survive in hostile environments and live off the land. Additional courses give them intense weapons and combat training.

One of the highlights of the Pipeline is a series of medical courses. The recruits learn basic first aid, followed by trauma medicine. Then they become adept at performing minor surgery. This includes treating stab and gunshot wounds. Considering the incredible array of skills these elite rescuers acquire, it is no wonder that their training is nicknamed "superman school."

A Special Warfare Combatant-craft Crewman (SWCC) from Special Boat Team 12 treats an injured teammate during a casualty assistance and evacuation scenario at the Naval Special Warfare Center in Coronado, California. The scenario covered basic first aid and advanced life-saving skills commonly used to treat combat-related injuries, as part of unit-level training.

The "Big Deal" Department

Air Force Master Sargeant Pat McKenna described a fairly typical incident in the Pipeline's combat diving course:

Airman Jason Cunningham

Jason Cunningham's body begged for air. Submerged 9 feet under, the airman's lungs prickled and burned, [as] every instinct urged him to burst to the surface and suck in cool, fresh air. But he ignored the red alert blaring in his brain and stayed below for several minutes. Soon [the recruit] lost consciousness and sank to the bottom of the pool. Immediately, a group of rugged men . . . [wearing] scuba gear hauled him out of the pool and revived him. . . . "No big deal," [Cunningham said]. No big deal? For most people, drowning ranks pretty high in the "big deal" department, right up there with . . . being buried alive. But Cunningham isn't what you'd call most people. He's going through the toughest school on the planet in hopes of becoming an Air Force pararescueman.

A student exits the 9D6 dunker during a simulated aircraft water landing exercise at the Aviation Survival Training Center at the Naval Air Station, in Jacksonville, Florida.

fact BOX

Showing Off in the "Dunker"

According to some Pipeline instructors, a few of the more fit recruits sometimes show off in the "dunker." This device tosses them upside-down into a freezing-cold pool, where they must hold their breath for more than a minute. The showoffs typically try to hold it much longer.

Students assigned to Basic Underwater Demolition/SEAL (BUD/S) class 286 participate in a surf passage training exercise at the Naval Amphibious Base, Coronado. Surf passage is one of many physically demanding evolutions that are part of First Phase training at BUD/S.

CHAPTER FOUR

Rescue AIRCRAFT, BOATS, and GEAR

To save the lives of injured people trapped in dangerous situations, rescuers must be well-trained and brave. The U.S. military's special ops rescuers possess these qualities in abundance. But such specialized, hazardous work requires more. The rescuers need an assortment of equally specialized support devices and gear. These include vehicles, especially planes and helicopters, for getting the rescuers to the victims; boats and scuba equipment for sea rescues; parachutes, weapons, and more. The Air Force pararescuemen and other military rescue personnel are highly adept in the use of such devices.

SPECIALIZED AIRPLANES

Among the many vehicles employed by pararescuemen, airplanes are particularly important. They are the fastest means of carrying the rescuers and their specialized equipment to the target areas. The Air Force's elite rescuers are part of the U.S. Air Force Special Operations Command (AFSOC). Its main base is at Hurlburt Field, near Fort Walton Beach, Florida. The base houses not only the rescuers, other personnel, and headquarters buildings, but also specialized rescue aircraft. These are maintained by the 16th Special Operations Wing (SOW), part of AFSOC.

The SOW operates by far the most popular and accomplished air transport used by the PJs and other special ops units. It is the C-130 Hercules transport, which first appeared in the 1950s. After that, the military developed numerous different versions of the plane.

One of the C-130s frequently used by pararescuemen is the MC-130 Combat Talon gunship. It has many advanced features. These include special sensors and tracking devices that help the pilots locate the people in need of rescuing. High-tech radar, infrared detectors, global positioning systems (GPS), and TV cameras are only a few of these devices. The Talon gunship also features jamming equipment, which can disrupt enemy communications. This quite often allows these planes to fly in and out of enemy territory without being detected.

As reflected in its name, the Talon gunship is also designed for combat. Like other C-130s, it carries powerful machine guns, missiles, and other weapons. In some situations, after the plane delivers the rescuers to the target area they come under enemy fire. If so, the pilot can double back and open fire on the enemy positions. This is one form of what the military calls close air support.

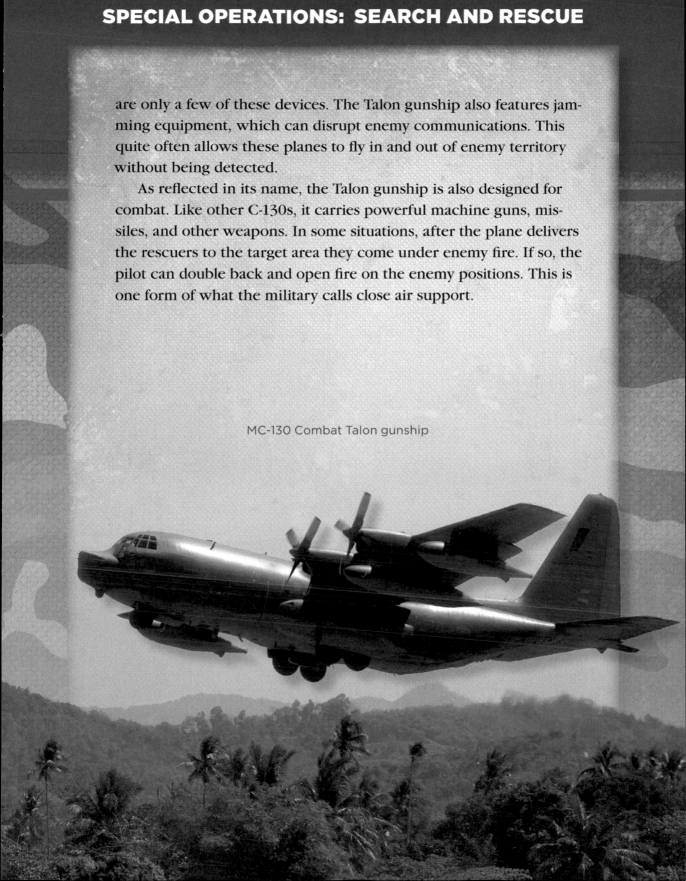

MC-130 Combat Talon gunship

FROM HALF-HELICOPTER TO HELICOPTER

The C-130s are not the only planes used for special ops rescues. A growing number of pararescue commandos are now using the V-22 Osprey. It flies like a plane but lands vertically like a helicopter. That makes it a sort of half-helicopter. The Osprey can fly at 316 mph (509 kmph) at sea level, and even faster at higher altitudes. It can go up to 1,011 miles (1,627 km) before needing to refuel. This makes it effective for carrying rescuers to remote places located well beyond the nearest U.S. airfield.

Along with the half-helicopter Osprey, Air Force pararescuemen use actual helicopters. The most popular is the HH-60 Pave Hawk. It is a special ops version of the Army's Black Hawk, made famous in the book and movie *Black Hawk Down.* (Coast Guard rescue units often use a different Black Hawk offshoot—the HH-65A Dolphin.) The Pave Hawk carries more fuel than a Black Hawk. So the Pave Hawk is better suited for long-distance missions like some undertaken by Air Force special ops rescuers.

Aviation boatswain's mates observe a V-22 Osprey as it launches from the flight deck aboard amphibious assault ship USS *Iwo Jima*.

The Pave Hawk's Rescue Hoist

The Pave Hawk helicopter was specially designed for use by special ops personnel. Among them are the pararescuemen employed by the Air Force. The versatile vehicle is equipped with portable radios, ropes and other climbing gear, rifles and other weapons, medical equipment, medicines, and many other items that the rescuers might need on a mission. The Pave Hawk is also equipped with a special rescue hoist. It consists of a sturdy cable-like device that can lift and hold up to 600 pounds (272 kg). A pararescuman can and often does use the hoist to lower himself to the ground. Later, he and the person he has rescued can use the cable to climb back aboard the helicopter. Or if the victim is unable to climb, the hoist can draw up a stretcher with him or her in it.

The Sikorsky HH-60 Pave Hawk is a Combat Search and Rescue (CSAR) helicopter derivative of the Sikorsky S-70 family. The Pave Hawk's primary function is to conduct day or night CSAR operations in hostile environments to recover downed aircrew or other isolated personnel during war.

INSTANT BOATS AND OTHER GEAR

Both the planes and helicopters used by the elite pararescue units are equipped with the latest portable rescue gear. One of the more useful examples is the RAMZ. The letters are short for Rigging Alternate Method Zodiac. It consists of a package containing a small un-inflated boat that one or more rescuers can inflate if needed in a sea mission. One official observer wrote, "Instead of being inflated during the parachute drop, the inflatable, motorized Zodiac boat is deflated and bundled up into a 4-foot cube, then parachuted out of a C-130. The engine, fuel, and medical equipment are also in the package. Two cargo parachutes are attached."

Air Force Guardian Angels from the 103rd Rescue Squadron, 106th Rescue Wing, gather at a Rigging Alternate Method Zodiac kit after their jump and get the Zodiac under way.

Other devices and items used by special ops rescuers vary according to where the missions take place. Whereas the RAMZ is helpful for water rescues, climbing gear is essential for missions in mountainous areas. Clothes covered with camouflage are also sometimes used. Their multicolors and patterns help to make a rescuer blend with jungle and desert settings.

In addition, parachutes can deliver rescuers into any terrain or environment where planes, cars, and other vehicles cannot go. A radio, night-vision goggles, and other gear add to the rescuers' considerable load. But those committed individuals believe it is crucial to be prepared for any situation. Having or not having a single item might be the difference between life and death for either the rescued individual or the rescuer himself.

fact BOX

Armored Vests

In missions in which a pararescue team goes into enemy territory, its members wear armored vests. These are frequently composed of Kevlar, a human-made fiber five times stronger than steel. Bullets from several kinds of small firearms cannot penetrate it.

A Navy SEAL freefalls from an Austrian C-130 aircraft above the Arctic Circle during Cold Response 2010. Cold Response is a Norwegian exercise open to all NATO nations for winter warfare and joint coalition training.

CHAPTER FIVE

The
Special Ops
RESCUERS
in ACTION

A Pave Hawk helicopter assigned to the 66th Rescue Squadron maneuvers behind an HC-130 to perform a helicopter air refueling exercise during Angel Thunder, the world's largest combat search and rescue exercise, in 2011.

The Air Force's PJs and other U.S. special ops rescuers have carried out thousands of missions over the years. Some of these were in and around the United States. Others occurred overseas during wars like those in Vietnam, Panama, Iraq, and Afghanistan. All of the people whose lives were saved in those missions have one thing in common. Their rescuers risked their own lives to save theirs. And on occasion, sadly, a rescuer made the ultimate sacrifice and never made it home.

A TYPICAL MISSION

Most of the missions of the elite military rescuers are small-scale. They typically involve one or two pilots, soldiers, or civilians who are injured or otherwise in trouble. As a rule, one, two, or three planes or helicopters respond. In them are skeleton crews and a handful of highly trained rescuers. Just such a mission is described here by former federal agent Nick Jacobellis:

> A U.S. Air Force pilot bailed out of his stricken aircraft over Serbia [in southern Europe] in 1999. [Two U.S.] Pave Low helicopters and one Pave Hawk helicopter transported two PJs and [another special ops member] through Serbian rocket and small-arms fire to rescue the pilot behind enemy lines. [The] downed pilot was safely extracted from behind enemy lines and onboard the Pave Hawk helicopter. [Even then] one of his rescuers physically covered him with his own body to further protect [him] from possible harm. [Mean]while, the flight of three U.S. Air Force helicopters returned to friendly airspace. This entire combat rescue operation is a perfect example of the PJ [rescue] mission.

AN EXAMPLE FOR OTHERS

Now and then, however, the Air Force pararescue jumpers encounter missions featuring unusual scope, complexity, and human courage.

Such a mission occurred in March 2002. Its highlight was the uncommon dedication and bravery of a twenty-six-year-old PJ—Jason Cunningham. He set an inspiring example of professionalism for rescuers of all kinds everywhere.

The mission took place soon after the infamous 9/11 terror attack on New York and Washington, D.C., in September 2001. The United States reacted by sending troops to Afghanistan. That is where members of the terrorist group, al-Qaeda, had planned and trained for the attack. The Americans quickly drove the terrorists from their bases. They fled to a valley in a remote sector of Afghanistan.

On March 4, 2002, a U.S. helicopter flew to Takur Ghar, a mountain on the edge of the valley. Its mission was to insert a small team of Navy SEALs. Their orders were to observe the enemy's positions and report back. Before the drop occurred, however, a nest of al-Qaeda fighters opened fire on the chopper. In the commotion, one of the SEALs, Neil Roberts, fell out. Only later, when the chopper was approaching the American base, did anyone realize he was missing.

Roberts' fellow special ops fighters swiftly conceived a plan to go back and rescue him. They did not know he had already been killed while resisting swarms of al-Qaeda fighters. Several U.S. commandos, including PJ Jason Cunningham, returned to Takur Ghar. There, they got into a fierce battle with the al-Qaeda forces.

U.S. Air Force Staff Sergeant Bill Cenna, a 212th Rescue Squadron pararescueman, prepares to move a simulated patient on a litter during training at Joint Base Elmendorf-Richardson in Alaska.

At first, Cunningham remained on his chopper and treated the wounds sustained by the other Americans. But then the vehicle was hit by an enemy missile and caught fire. So Cunningham decided to move the wounded to a safer location outside the chopper. One by one, he helped them out. This required exposing himself to al-Qaeda bullets, which exploded all around him. Each time he went back to grab the next patient, he fired his own weapon at the faceless enemy.

Finally all the wounded were out of the chopper. But the al-Qaeda bullets and mortar rounds now became even more intense. This forced Cunningham to move his patients again. A military spokesman told what happened to him next:

> Shortly after noon, [he] was hit just below his body armor. His liver was shattered, and he was bleeding internally. Despite the pain, he continued to direct patient movement. . . . [He] slowly bled to death on the mountaintop. . . . About 8 p.m. Cunningham became the first pararescue jumper to die in combat since the Vietnam War. His selfless actions saved the lives of ten gravely wounded Americans but cost his own.

Like Jason Cunningham, all of the U.S. military's elite rescuers know they run the risk of dying in the line of duty. But their desire to help others outweighs their concerns for themselves. To them, their motto—"that others may live"—is not merely a group of empty words. It is a blueprint for a courageous, worthwhile profession. By choosing it, a handful of valiant men have given thousands of others a precious second chance at life.

fact BOX

(*From left to right*) Technical Sergeant Keary Miller, Senior Airman Jason Cunningham, and Staff Sergeant Gabe Brown about three weeks before the Battle at Takur Ghar

In His Memory

Jason Cunningham's heroism and sacrifice moved all members of the U.S. special ops community. To honor his memory, the Air Force posthumously awarded him the Air Force Cross, its highest honor. It was only the second time this award was presented since the Vietnam War.

0028

050028

USAF

Source Notes

Chapter 1: A Daring Rescue Above the Clouds

p. 11,   "my hairiest mission," Jack Brehm, "Saving Lives at 26,000 Feet," interview by Geoff Metcalf, http://www.geoffmetcalf.com/qa/19624.html.

p. 12,   "It took us 11 hours . . ." Ibid.

p. 12,   "The temperature was going down . . ." Ibid.

pp. 12-13, "There is a fine line . . ." Ibid.

Chapter 2: America's Elite Rescue Units

p. 23,   "Pararescue is the singular . . ." John Cassidy, "Pararescue History," http://www.specialtactics.com/history.shtml.

p. 24,   "We want to get in . . ." Master Sargeant Pat McKenna, "Superman School," http://www.militaryspot.com/career/featured_military_jobs/.

p. 24,   "Being part of this team . . ." Robert L. LaPointe, "Want to Be a PJ?," http://www.pjsinnam.com/join_pararescue.htm.

p. 26,   "The ultimate goal . . ." U.S. Coast Guard, "SAR Program Information," http://www.uscg.mil/hq/cg5/cg534/SAR_Program_Info.asp.

Chapter 3: Graduating from Superman School

p. 30,   "'The Pipeline' is . . ." Brehm, "Saving Lives at 26,000 Feet."

p. 31,   "We want to break . . ." McKenna, "Superman School."

p. 33,   "Pool Week runs . . ." Ibid.

p. 36,   "Jason Cunningham's body . . ." Ibid.

Chapter 4: Rescue Aircraft, Boats, and Gear

p. 46,   "Instead of being inflated . . ." Aero-New Network, "Pararescue Team Trains for Shuttle Launch Recovery," http://www.aero-news.net/ANNTicker.cfm?do=main.textpost&id=d48cdc7e-7624-44fe-af0b-647d4b8ccc68.

Chapter 5: The Special Ops Rescuers in Action

p. 51,   "A U.S. Air Force pilot . . ." Nick Jacobellis, "Pararescue Jumpers," http://www.tactical-life.com/online/tactical-weapons/pararescue-jumpers/.

p. 54,   "Shortly after noon . . ." American Veterans Center, "Senior Airman Jason Cunningham, USAF," http://www.americanveteranscenter.org/events/conference/awards/paul-ray-smith-award/senior-airman-jason-cunningham-usaf/.

Glossary

camouflage: Patterns and colors designed to make military uniforms, gear, and weapons blend in with a given natural setting.

chopper: A nickname for a helicopter.

civilian: A person who is not in the armed forces.

close air support: Aid given to ground fighters by planes and helicopters.

commando: An elite, specially trained soldier who is assigned to difficult, dangerous missions.

firefight: A battle involving firearms.

GPS (Global Positioning System): A network of orbiting satellites that allow people to quickly compute their exact position on Earth's surface.

hoist: A device for lifting things.

hostage: A person who is held somewhere against his or her will.

insert: A military term meaning to place one or more persons in a given location.

Kevlar: A rugged cloth-like material that is five times stronger than steel.

mortar: A small artillery piece or cannon.

NASA: The official U.S. space agency.

navigation: Methods of finding one's location and plotting the way from one place to another.

Pararescueman: A U.S. Air Force commando who rescues people who are injured or otherwise in trouble.

PJ: Short for "Pararescue Jumper," or Pararescueman.

posthumous: After death.

RAMZ: A package containing a small inflatable boat for use in sea rescues.

recruit: A soldier, sailor, or other fighter who is in training.

SAR: A common acronym (group of letters standing for something) for "Search and Rescue."

special ops: Short for Special Operations Forces, consisting of the U.S. military's elite units of soldiers.

Bibliography

Brehm, Jack, and Pete Nelson. *That Others May Live: The True Story of the PJs*. New York: Three Rivers Press, 2001.

Day, Dwayne A. "Search and Rescue Helicopters." http://www.centennialofflight.gov/essay/Rotary/SAR/HE9.htm.

Drury, Bob. *The Rescue Season: The Heroic Story of Parajumpers on the Edge of the World*. Thorndile, MN: Thorndike Press, 2001.

Ewing, Philip. "The Inside Story of the Alaska Ranger Rescue." http://www.navytimes.com/news/2008/05/coastguard_ranger_rescue_051908w/.

Labrecque, Ellen. *Special Forces*. Mankrato, MN: Heinemann-Raintree, 2012.

Lewan, Todd. *The Last Run: A True Story of Rescue and Redemption on the Alaska Seas*. New York: HarperCollins, 2004.

Montana, Jack. *Elite Forces Selection*. Broomall, PA: Mason Crest, 2011.

———. *Navy SEALs*. Broomall, PA: Mason Crest, 2011.

Nelson, Drew. *Green Berets*. New York: Gareth Stevens, 2012.

Pushies, Fred J. *Special Ops: America's Elite Forces in 21st Century Combat*. St. Paul: MBI, 2003.

Roller, William. "Marine Corps Air Station Search and Rescue." http://www.yumasun.com/articles/station-48067-air-corps.html.

Roza, Greg. *Careers in the Coast Guard's Search and Rescue Units*. New York: Rosen, 2003.

Sample, Doug. "Coast Guard Search and Rescue." http://usmilitary.about.com/od/coastguard/a/cgsearch.htm.

Sandler, Michael. *Pararescumen in Action*. New York: Bearport, 2008.

Smith, Stew. "Air Force Pararescue Jumper Training." http://www.military.com/military-fitness/air-force-special-operations/air-force-para-rescue.

Von Wormer, Nicholas. *The Ultimate Air Force Basic Training Guidebook*. El Dorado Hills, CA: Savas Beatie, 2010.

Whitcomb, Darrell D. *Combat Search and Rescue in Desert Storm*. Maxwell AF Base, AL: Air University Press, 2006.

Web sites

Official Web site of the Navy SEALs and SWCC
http://www.sealswcc.com/

U.S.A.F. Pararescue. "Superman School."
http://www.pararescue.com/unitinfo.aspx?id=490

Organizing for Search and Rescue
http://www.airpower.au.af.mil/airchronicles/apj/apj95/sum95_files/
meggett.htm

Pararescue History
http://www.pararescue.com/history.aspx?id=449

Weapons of the Special Forces
http://www.popularmechanics.com/technology/military/1281576

U.S. Air Force. Fact Sheet for the CV-22 Osprey.
http://www.af.mil/information/factsheets/factsheet.asp?fsID=3668

Index

Photo Credits